THE INDIAN SPIRITUALITY FOR CHILDREN

AN INTRODUCTION TO INDIA'S SPIRITUAL AND CULTURAL HERITAGE FOR CHILDREN

DR. JAGADEESH PILLAI

|| Dedicated to all wisdom seekers around the world ||

&

Contents

Contents

Prayer

**"Om Bhadram Karnebhih Shrunuyaama
DevaahBhadram Pashyemaakshabhiryajatraah
SthirairangaistushtuvaamsastanoobhihVyashema
Devahitam YadaayuhSwasti Na Indro
VridhashravaahSwasti Nah Pooshaa
VishwavedaahSwasti Nastaarkshyo ArishtanemihSwasti
No Brihaspatir DadhaatuOm Shantih, Shantih, Shantih"**

The literal meaning of this mantra is: OM. O Gods! Let us
hear auspicious words from our ears. O reverent Gods! Let
us behold propitious visions from our eyes, let our organs
and body be stable, healthy, and strong. Let us do that
which is pleasing to the gods in the life span allotted to us.
May Indra, inscribed in the scriptures, bring us fortune!
May Pushan, the knower of the world, grant us prosperity!
May Trakshya, who vanquishes enemies, bestow us with
blessings! May Brihaspati bring us success!
OM Peace, Peace, Peace.

About The Author

Dr. Jagadeesh Pillai is a renowned Guinness World Record holder, writer, and researcher hailing from Varanasi, also known as the abode of Lord Shiva. With a Ph.D. in Vedic Science and a range of creative ideas and achievements, he is a true polymath. He is the author of more than 100 books including Research Publications. Although his roots can be traced back to Kerala, the people of Varanasi hold him in high regard and affectionately consider him one of their own.

Dr. Pillai has achieved four Guinness World Records in the following subjects:

"Script to Screen" - In this record, Dr. Pillai produced and directed an animation film within the shortest time possible, breaking the previous record set by Canadians. He has also received numerous national and international awards and recognitions for this achievement.

Longest Line of Postcards - For this record, Dr. Pillai created a line of 16,300 postcards on the occasion of the 163rd anniversary of Indian Postal Day. The event also included a questionnaire about the Indian flag.

Largest Poster Awareness Campaign - Dr. Pillai designed an awareness campaign on the subject of "Beti Bachao - Beti Padhao" (Save the Girl Child - Educate the Girl Child) to achieve this record.

Largest Envelope - In tribute to the Indian Prime Minister's

"Make in India" initiative, Dr. Pillai created a 4000 square meter envelope using waste paper to achieve this record.

Attempted - **70000 Candles on a 210 kg Cake** - To celebrate the 70th Indian Independence Day, Dr. Pillai attempted to light 70,000 candles on a 210 kg cake, which was recorded in World Records India.

Attempted - **Documentary on Dhamek Stupa of Sarnath in 17 Languages** - Dr. Pillai attempted to create a documentary on the Dhamek Stupa of Sarnath, dubbing it in 17 different languages. The result of this attempt is currently awaiting confirmation from the Guinness World Records.

Dr. Pillai is skilled in teaching the Bhagavad Gita, a Hindu scripture, and is popular among young people. He has helped many young people improve their lives through his motivational teachings.

In addition to teaching, he has composed and sung numerous Sanskrit Bhajans and patriotic songs.

He has also written and directed several short films and documentaries for awareness campaigns, and has volunteered with the police in both UP and Kerala to spread awareness about various issues through videos and photography.

Incredibly, he has produced and directed over 100 documentaries about the city of Varanasi, all on his own.

He has also helped and guided more than 25 boys and girls to achieve world records through creative and innovative methods. He is a multifaceted person who uses his intellect and the blessings given to him by God to excel in various areas. He is both a teacher and a student, always learning and teaching, and is able to master any subject he comes across.

He is a selfless social activist and motivational speaker who has overcome struggles and failures to become a successful and enthusiastic individual with a rich life experience.

In addition to his work with the Bhagavad Gita, he is also an efficient Tarot card reader, Astro-Vastu consultant, and a talented singer and composer. He has sung the entire Ram Charita Manas and Bhagavad Gita in his own compositions, and has sung the phrase "Lokah Samastha Sukhino Bhavantu" in 50 different languages. He is currently working on a detailed and scientific study of Vedas, Upanishads, Puranas, and the Bhagavad Gita. He has also composed and sung the Hanuman Chalisa and Gayatri Mantra in 108 and 1008 different compositions, respectively.

Awards - Four Times Guinness World Records, Winner of Mahatma Gandhi Vishwa Shanti Puraskar, Mahatma Gandhi Global Peace Ambassador, Kashi Ratna Award, Dr. APJ Abdul Kalam Motivational Person of the Year 2017, Mother Teresa Award, Indira Gandhi Priyadarshini Award, Bharat Vikas Ratna Award, Udyog Ratna Award, Vigyan Prasar Award, Poorvanchal Ratn Samman.

PREFACE

Indian spirituality has been an important part of Indian culture for thousands of years. It is an incredibly complex and diverse set of beliefs and practices that have been shaped by the many different religions, philosophies, and cultures of India. This book, The Indian Spirituality for Children: An Introduction to India's Spiritual and Cultural Heritage for Children, seeks to explore Indian spirituality and its significance for children.

This book is intended to serve as an introduction to the rich history and culture of Indian spirituality for readers who are new to the subject. It explores the various religions and philosophies that make up Indian spirituality, their significance for children, and their impact on education, mental health, and contemporary society. It also examines the role of Indian spirituality in the future and how it can be used to foster positive growth and development in children.

The book draws on research from a variety of sources, including interviews with key figures in the Indian spirituality industry, archival materials, and cultural analysis. I have also conducted extensive field research in India, including attending spiritual events, interviewing spiritual teachers, and visiting locations associated with the practice of Indian spirituality. Through this research, I hope to provide readers with a comprehensive understanding of the Indian spirituality industry and its various components.

I am deeply passionate about the art of Indian spirituality and hope that this book will help to spread the appreciation of this wonderful form of belief and practice. I believe that Indian spirituality has a great deal to offer to children and I am excited to share its cultural and historical significance with my readers.

I

Introduction to Indian Spirituality

India is a land steeped in spirituality, with a rich and diverse tradition that has evolved over thousands of years. Indian spirituality is a way of understanding the world and one's place in it, and it encompasses a wide range of beliefs, practices, and philosophies.

At its core, Indian spirituality is based on the belief that the ultimate reality is one of oneness, and that all living things are connected. It teaches that the ultimate goal of human existence is to realize this oneness and to achieve a state of inner peace, happiness, and liberation from the cycle of birth and death.

Indian spirituality encompasses a wide range of practices and traditions, including yoga, meditation, Ayurveda, and various forms of worship. Yoga is a physical and spiritual practice that aims to unite the mind, body, and spirit, and it includes postures, breathing techniques, and meditation. Meditation is a practice that helps to still the mind and to achieve a state of inner peace and clarity. Ayurveda is a traditional system of medicine that focuses on maintaining balance and harmony within the body.

Hinduism, Buddhism, Jainism, Sikhism, Sufism are some of the major religions that are practiced in India and they all have a rich spiritual heritage. Each of these religions has its own unique beliefs, practices, and philosophies, and they all offer a path to spiritual growth and self-discovery.

Indian spirituality also places a strong emphasis on the importance of living in harmony with nature and the environment. Many spiritual practices, such as yoga and meditation, encourage individuals to develop a deeper connection with the natural world. Additionally, many spiritual practices, such as Ayurveda, are based on the belief that health and well-being are closely connected to our environment.

Furthermore, Indian spirituality also places a strong emphasis on the importance of community and social responsibility. Many spiritual practices, such as acts of devotion and charity, encourage individuals to work together for the greater good.

Indian spirituality is a vast and diverse tradition that encompasses a wide range of beliefs, practices, and philosophies. It is based on the belief that the ultimate reality is one of oneness, and that all living things are connected. The ultimate goal of Indian spirituality is to realize this oneness and to achieve a state of inner peace, happiness, and liberation from the cycle of birth and death. This spiritual tradition encompasses a wide range of practices and traditions, including yoga, meditation, Ayurveda, and various forms of worship, and it encourages individuals to live in harmony with nature, the environment and the society.

"Indian spirituality is the path to understanding our true nature and realizing our full potential."

৪৩

II

The Significance of Indian Spirituality in Children

Indian spirituality is a rich and ancient tradition that offers valuable lessons and insights for individuals of all ages, including children. Introducing children to Indian spirituality can have a profound and positive impact on their development, both emotionally and spiritually.

Firstly, Indian spirituality teaches children the value of self-awareness and self-reflection. Through practices such as yoga and meditation, children learn to quiet their minds and to focus on the present moment. This can help them to develop emotional intelligence and to become more resilient in the face of stress and adversity.

Secondly, Indian spirituality encourages children to develop a sense of gratitude and compassion. Many spiritual practices, such as acts of devotion and charity, teach children the importance of helping others and of living in harmony with the community. This can help children to become more empathetic and compassionate individuals.

Thirdly, Indian spirituality teaches children the importance of living in harmony with nature and the environment. Many spiritual practices, such as yoga and meditation, encourage children to develop a deeper connection with the natural world. This can help children to become more environmentally conscious and to appreciate the beauty and wonder of the world around them.

Lastly, Indian spirituality can help children to develop a sense of purpose and meaning in their lives. Through spiritual practices such as yoga and meditation, children can learn to understand their place in the world and to find meaning and purpose in their lives.

Indian spirituality has significant value to children, it can help to develop self-awareness, compassion, environmental consciousness and sense of purpose. It is important for adults to introduce children to Indian spirituality in an age-appropriate way, to help them develop a lifelong appreciation for the wisdom and teachings of this ancient tradition.

"Through Indian spirituality, we learn to live in harmony with nature and the environment."

ॐ

III

Hinduism and Indian Spirituality

Hinduism is one of the oldest and most diverse religions in the world, and it is also an integral part of Indian spirituality. Hinduism has its roots in ancient India and it is based on a complex system of beliefs, practices, and philosophies.

One of the key beliefs in Hinduism is the concept of Brahman, which is the ultimate reality and the source of all things. Hinduism teaches that the ultimate goal of human existence is to realize the oneness of the individual self with Brahman, which is also referred to as Self-realization or enlightenment.

Hinduism also teaches the concept of karma, which is the belief that one's actions in this life will determine their fate in the next life. Hinduism also stresses the importance of living in harmony with nature and the environment.

Hinduism includes a wide range of spiritual practices and traditions, such as yoga, meditation, and various forms of worship. Yoga and meditation are an integral part of Hinduism, and they are believed to help individuals to achieve a state of inner peace, happiness, and spiritual enlightenment.

Hinduism also includes a wide range of gods and goddesses, each with their own unique characteristics and roles. These gods and goddesses are revered and worshiped in temples, shrines, and homes, and they are believed to have the power to grant blessings and to remove obstacles.

Hinduism also includes a wide range of spiritual texts, including the Vedas, the Upanishads, the Bhagavad Gita, and the Ramayana. These texts are considered to be sacred and they offer guidance and wisdom for individuals on their spiritual journey.

Hinduism is an integral part of Indian spirituality and it has played a significant role in shaping the culture, traditions, and beliefs of India. Hinduism emphasizes on the ultimate goal of human existence is to realize the oneness of the individual self with Brahman, it stresses on the importance of living in harmony with nature and the environment, it includes a wide range of spiritual practices and traditions, and it has a rich tradition of spiritual texts that offer guidance and wisdom for individuals on their spiritual journey.

ॐ

"Indian spirituality teaches us to find inner
peace and balance in a fast-paced and stressful
world."

ॐ

IV

Buddhism and Indian Spirituality

Buddhism is a major world religion that originated in ancient India, and it is also an important aspect of Indian spirituality. The teachings of Buddhism are based on the life and teachings of Siddhartha Gautama, also known as the Buddha, who lived and taught in India more than 2,500 years ago.

One of the key teachings of Buddhism is the Four Noble Truths, which state that suffering is an inherent part of human existence, that the cause of suffering is desire and attachment, that it is possible to end suffering, and that the path to the end of suffering is the Eightfold Path. The Eightfold Path is a set of guidelines for living a virtuous and ethical life, including right understanding, right intention, right speech, right action, right livelihood, right effort, right mindfulness, and right concentration.

Buddhism also teaches the concept of non-attachment and the importance of living in the present moment. Through the practice of mindfulness and meditation, individuals can learn to let go of desires and attachments and to focus on the present moment.

Buddhism also places a strong emphasis on compassion and altruism. The practice of compassion and altruism is believed to bring about inner peace and happiness, as well as to improve the lives of others.

Buddhism includes a wide range of spiritual practices and traditions, such as meditation, mindfulness, and various forms of worship. Meditation and mindfulness are an integral part of Buddhism, and they are believed to help individuals to achieve a state of inner peace, happiness, and spiritual enlightenment.

Buddhism also includes a wide range of spiritual texts, including the Pali Canon and the Mahayana sutras. These texts offer guidance and wisdom for individuals on their spiritual journey.

Buddhism is an important aspect of Indian spirituality and it has had a significant impact on the culture, traditions, and beliefs of India. Buddhism emphasizes on the Four Noble Truths, the Eightfold Path, non-attachment and the importance of living in the present moment. It stresses on the importance of compassion and altruism, and encourages the practice of mindfulness and meditation to achieve inner peace and enlightenment. Buddhism also has a rich tradition of spiritual texts that offer guidance and wisdom for individuals on their spiritual journey. It's teachings have been influencing many other spiritual traditions in India, and have become an integral part of Indian spiritual heritage.

*"The spiritual practices of Indian spirituality
are the key to unlocking the power of the mind
and the soul."*

ॐ

V
Sikhism and Indian Spirituality

Sikhism is a monotheistic religion founded in the 15th century in the Punjab region of India, and it is also an important aspect of Indian spirituality. The teachings of Sikhism are based on the teachings and writings of Guru Nanak, the first Sikh guru, and his nine successive gurus.

One of the key teachings of Sikhism is the belief in one eternal and formless God, who is the creator, sustainer and destroyer of all. The ultimate goal of human existence in Sikhism is to merge with the eternal God and achieve liberation from the cycle of rebirths.

Sikhism also teaches the importance of leading an honest and virtuous life, and the importance of serving others. The practice of selfless service, known as seva, is seen as a way to connect with God and to attain spiritual growth.

Sikhism also places a strong emphasis on the importance of meditation and the recitation of God's name, known as naam japna. This practice is believed to bring about inner peace and to help individuals to focus on the present moment.

Sikhism includes a wide range of spiritual practices and traditions, such as meditation, singing of hymns, and various forms of worship. Meditation is an integral part of Sikhism and it is believed to help individuals to achieve a state of inner peace and spiritual enlightenment. The singing of hymns, known as kirtan, is also a central aspect of Sikh worship and it is believed to bring about a connection with God.

Sikhism also includes a wide range of spiritual texts, including the Guru Granth Sahib, which is considered to be the living guru of the Sikhs. This text contains the teachings of the Sikh gurus and it offers guidance and wisdom for individuals on their spiritual journey.

Sikhism is an important aspect of Indian spirituality and it has had a significant impact on the culture, traditions and beliefs of India. Sikhism emphasizes on the belief in one eternal God, the ultimate goal of human existence is to merge with the eternal God, and the importance of leading an honest and virtuous life. The practice of selfless service, meditation, and the recitation of God's name is considered to be central to Sikh spirituality. Sikhism has a rich tradition of spiritual practices and traditions that are centered around devotional worship and it includes a wide range of spiritual texts that offer guidance and wisdom for individuals on their spiritual journey. Sikhism also stresses on the importance of community and social responsibility, which is a fundamental aspect of this spiritual tradition.

"Indian spirituality is the foundation of a meaningful and compassionate life."

ॐ

VI

Jainism and Indian Spirituality

Jainism is an ancient Indian religion that has its origins in the teachings of the Jina, or spiritual conquerors, who lived in ancient India. It is also an important aspect of Indian spirituality. The ultimate goal of Jainism is to achieve spiritual liberation, or moksha, and to escape the cycle of rebirths.

One of the key teachings of Jainism is the concept of non-violence, or ahimsa. Jains believe that all living beings have souls, and that it is wrong to harm any living being. This belief in non-violence extends to all aspects of life, including food choices, and many Jains are vegetarian.

Jainism also teaches the importance of self-control and self-discipline, and the importance of living a simple and modest life. Jains also follow the Five Great Vows (Mahavratas), which are non-violence, truthfulness, not stealing, celibacy, and non-possession.

Jainism includes a wide range of spiritual practices and traditions, such as meditation, fasting, and various forms of worship. Meditation is an integral part of Jainism, and it is believed to help individuals to achieve a state of inner peace, happiness, and spiritual enlightenment. Fasting is also a central aspect of Jainism, and it is believed to help individuals to control their desires and to purify the mind and body.

Jainism also includes a wide range of spiritual texts, including the Jain Agamas and the Jain Upanga. These texts offer guidance and wisdom for individuals on their spiritual journey.

Jainism is an important aspect of Indian spirituality and it has had a significant impact on the culture, traditions, and beliefs of India. Jainism emphasizes on the ultimate goal of achieving spiritual liberation and the importance of non-violence, self-control and self-discipline, and a simple and modest life. Jains follow the Five Great Vows, and it includes a wide range of spiritual practices and traditions, such as meditation and fasting. Jainism also has a rich tradition of spiritual texts that offer guidance and wisdom for individuals on their spiritual journey.

"Indian spirituality is the path to self-knowledge and self-discovery."

଼

VII

Sufism and Indian Spirituality

Sufism is a mystical Islamic tradition that originated in the Middle East and has a significant presence in India, and it is also an important aspect of Indian spirituality. Sufism emphasizes the personal, direct experience of God and the development of a close relationship with the divine.

One of the key teachings of Sufism is the concept of love and devotion to God, or Allah, and the importance of purifying the soul in order to attain closeness to God. This is achieved through practices such as meditation, prayer, and the recitation of the Quran.

Sufism also teaches the importance of self-discipline and self-control, and the importance of living a simple and modest life. Sufis believe that the path to spiritual enlightenment is through the purification of the self, and the renunciation of material possessions and desires.

Sufism includes a wide range of spiritual practices and traditions, such as meditation, prayer, and various forms of worship. Meditation is an integral part of Sufism, and it is believed to help individuals to achieve a state of inner peace, happiness, and spiritual enlightenment. Prayer and the recitation of the Quran is also a central aspect of Sufism, and it is believed to bring about a connection with God.

Sufism also includes a wide range of spiritual texts, including the poetry of Rumi, Hafiz, and other Sufi poets, which is considered to be central to Sufi spiritual practice and teaching. These texts offer guidance and wisdom for individuals on their spiritual journey.

Sufism is an important aspect of Indian spirituality and it has had a significant impact on the culture, traditions, and beliefs of India. Sufism emphasizes on the concept of love and devotion to God, the importance of purifying the soul, self-discipline, and self-control, and a simple and modest life. It includes a wide range of spiritual practices and traditions, such as meditation, prayer, and various forms of worship. Sufism also has a rich tradition of spiritual texts that offer guidance and wisdom for individuals on their spiritual journey.

"The teachings of Indian spirituality provide guidance on how to live a fulfilling and satisfying life."

VIII

Indian Spirituality and Education

Indian spirituality has had a profound impact on education in India, and it continues to shape the way in which education is approached and practiced in the country.

One of the key ways in which Indian spirituality has influenced education is through the emphasis on the development of the whole person, rather than just the intellect. Indian spirituality teaches that individuals have multiple dimensions to their being, including the physical, mental, emotional, and spiritual. Education in India, therefore, aims to nurture and develop all of these aspects of the individual, rather than just focusing on the intellect.

Another way in which Indian spirituality has influenced education is through the emphasis on the importance of self-knowledge, or atma-jnana. Indian spirituality teaches that individuals should strive to understand their true nature and to realize their full potential. Education in India, therefore, places a strong emphasis on the importance of self-reflection, self-awareness, and self-discovery.

Indian spirituality also stresses the importance of living in harmony with nature and the environment, and this is reflected in the emphasis on environmental education in Indian schools.

The spiritual practices such as Yoga, Meditation, and Pranayama are also being integrated in the curriculum of schools in India, as they are believed to help individuals to achieve a state of inner peace, happiness, and spiritual enlightenment.

Indian spirituality has had a significant impact on education in India, shaping the way in which education is approached and practiced. Indian spirituality emphasizes on the development of the whole person, the importance of self-knowledge and self-discovery, the importance of living in harmony with nature and the environment, and the integration of spiritual practices in the curriculum. This holistic approach to education is considered to be an important aspect of Indian spiritual heritage.

"Indian spirituality is the key to unlocking the secrets of the universe and the meaning of life."

ॐ

IX

Indian Spirituality and Mental Health

Indian spirituality has long been considered to be an important aspect of mental health and well-being in India. The spiritual practices, teachings, and philosophies of Indian spirituality have been used for centuries to promote mental health and to treat mental health disorders.

One of the key ways in which Indian spirituality has influenced mental health is through the emphasis on the importance of mindfulness and meditation. Indian spirituality teaches that the mind is the source of all suffering, and that through mindfulness and meditation, individuals can learn to control their thoughts and emotions and to achieve a state of inner peace. Mindfulness and meditation practices, such as yoga and pranayama, are believed to help individuals to reduce stress, anxiety, and depression.

Another way in which Indian spirituality has influenced mental health is through the emphasis on the importance of self-knowledge and self-discovery. Indian spirituality teaches that individuals should strive to understand their true nature and to realize their full potential. This emphasis on self-knowledge is believed to help individuals to develop a sense of self-worth, self-esteem and to foster resilience.

The spiritual practices and teachings of Indian spirituality also provide a sense of meaning and purpose to life, which is believed to be beneficial for mental health. The belief in something greater than oneself, the sense of connection to something beyond the self, and the understanding that one's actions have a broader impact are all considered to be important aspects of Indian spirituality that are believed to contribute to mental well-being.

Indian spirituality has had a significant impact on mental health in India. The emphasis on mindfulness, meditation, self-knowledge, self-discovery, and the sense of meaning and purpose provided by Indian spirituality are believed to be beneficial for mental health. The integration of spiritual practices such as yoga and pranayama in mental health treatment have been found to be effective in reducing stress, anxiety, and depression. Indian spirituality's holistic approach to mental health is considered to be an important aspect of Indian spiritual heritage.

*"The spiritual practices of Indian spirituality
are the key to good health and well-being."*

౬౩

X

Indian Spirituality and Contemporary Society

Indian spirituality has had a significant impact on contemporary society in India. The spiritual practices, teachings, and philosophies of Indian spirituality have been adopted and adapted by many individuals and communities in India to meet the challenges and opportunities of contemporary society.

One of the key ways in which Indian spirituality has influenced contemporary society is through the popularity of yoga and meditation. Yoga and meditation are believed to help individuals to achieve a state of inner peace and to reduce stress, anxiety, and depression. These practices have become increasingly popular in India and around the world, and they are now considered to be an integral part of contemporary society.

Another way in which Indian spirituality has influenced contemporary society is through the emphasis on environmental conservation and sustainability. Indian spirituality teaches that individuals should live in harmony with nature and the environment, and this emphasis has led to increased awareness and action on environmental issues in contemporary society.

Indian spirituality also stresses the importance of community and social responsibility. This is reflected in the growing popularity of volunteerism, philanthropy, and social enterprise in contemporary society.

In addition, Indian spirituality has also played a role in shaping the contemporary popular culture in India, from Bollywood movies to fashion, the influence of Indian spirituality can be seen in the way people live, think and consume.

Indian spirituality has had a significant impact on contemporary society in India. The popularity of yoga and meditation, the emphasis on environmental conservation and sustainability, the growing popularity of volunteerism, philanthropy, and social enterprise, and the influence on popular culture are all examples of how Indian spirituality has shaped and continues to shape contemporary society. The holistic approach of Indian spirituality, which encompasses not only the spiritual but also the physical, mental, emotional and environmental aspects, is considered to be an important aspect of Indian spiritual heritage.

*"Indian spirituality is the path to
enlightenment and self-realization."*

XI

Indian Spirituality and the Future

Indian spirituality has a rich history and heritage that has evolved over thousands of years and continues to shape the culture, traditions, and beliefs of India. As we look to the future, it is likely that Indian spirituality will continue to play an important role in shaping the lives of individuals and communities in India and around the world.

One of the key ways in which Indian spirituality is likely to shape the future is through its emphasis on personal and spiritual development. The spiritual practices and teachings of Indian spirituality, such as yoga, meditation, and pranayama, are believed to help individuals to achieve a state of inner peace, happiness, and spiritual enlightenment. As the world becomes increasingly fast-paced and stressful, it is likely that more and more people will turn to Indian spirituality to find inner peace and balance.

Another way in which Indian spirituality is likely to shape the future is through its emphasis on environmental conservation and sustainability. The teachings of Indian spirituality have always emphasized the importance of living in harmony with nature and the environment, and this emphasis is likely to become even more important in the future as the world faces increasing environmental challenges.

The future also sees the integration of Indian spirituality in healthcare and wellness, it has been found that spiritual practices such as yoga and meditation are effective in reducing stress, anxiety, and depression, and many healthcare professionals are now incorporating these practices into their treatments.

In addition, Indian spirituality is also likely to shape the future through its emphasis on community and social responsibility. As the world becomes increasingly interconnected and interdependent, it is likely that more and more people will turn to Indian spirituality for guidance on how to live a meaningful and compassionate life.

Indian spirituality has a rich history and heritage that has evolved over thousands of years and continues to shape the culture, traditions, and beliefs of India. As we look to the future, it is likely that Indian spirituality will continue to play an important role in shaping the lives of individuals and communities in India and around the world. Indian spirituality's emphasis on personal and spiritual development, environmental conservation, community and social responsibility, and integration in healthcare and wellness is likely to shape the future in a positive way. It is considered to be an important aspect of Indian spiritual heritage.

"Through Indian spirituality, we learn to appreciate the beauty and wonder of the world around us."

૭૩

OTHER BOOKS OF THE AUTHOR

1. The Moments When I Met God
2. Kashiyile Theertha Pathangal
3. GURU GYAN VANI
4. Abhiprerak Gita
5. ASSI SE JAIN GHAT TAK
6. Hopelessness of Arjuna
7. The Soul and It's True Nature
8. Sense of Action (Karma)
9. Action through Wisdom
10. Action through Wisdom
11. THEORY AND PRACTICAL OF EVERY ACTION
12. LOGICAL UNDERSTANDING OF THE SUPREME
13. THE IMPERISHABLE SUPREME
14. Yatra Nishadraj se Hanuman Ghat Tak
15. Yatra Karnatak Ghat se Raja Ghat Tak
16. Yatra Pandey Ghat se Prayagraj Ghat Tak
17. Yatra Ranjendra Prasad Ghat se Dattatreya Ghat Tak
18. YaatraSindhiya Ghat se Gwaliar Ghat Tak
19. Yatra Mangala Gauri Ghat se Hanuman Gadhi Ghat Tak
20. Yatra Gaay Ghat Se Nishad Ghat Tak
21. MAA GANGA, GHATEN EVM UTSAV
22. Ganga Arti Dev Deepavali evam Any Utsav
23. Potentials of Digitalized India
24. VEDIC CONSCIOUSNESS
25. A Brief Introduction to Vedic Science
26. Kashi ke Barah Jyotirling
27. IMPACT OF MOTIVATION
28. Let's have a Milky Way Journey
29. Color Therapy in a Nutshell

30. Rigveda in a Nutshell
31. Yajurveda in a Nutshell
32. Samveda in a Nutshell
33. Atharva Veda in a Nutshell
34. Ayushman Bhava - Ayurveda
35. Srimad Bhagavad Gita and Upanishad Connection
36. Srimad Bhagavad Gita - an attempt to summarize each chapter.
37. Facts and Impact of Nakshatra
38. Astro Gems - NAVARATNA
39. Ekadashi - A Concise Overview
40. A Concise View of Hanuman Chalisa
41. Inspirational Gita
42. Nakshatraranyam
43. Summary of 18 Mahapuranas
44. Synopsis of 18 Upa Puranas
45. Rigvediya Upanishads
46. Shukla Yajurvediya Upanishads
47. Krishna Yajurvediya Upanishads
48. Samavediya Upanishads
49. Atharvavediya Upanishads
50. The Seven Great Sages
51. From Rocket Scientist to President Dr. APJ Abdul Kalam
52. The Visionary's Voice - Quotes of Dr. APJ Abdul Kalam
53. The Wisdom of Swami Vivekananda: Insights and Inspiration from a Legendary Spiritual Teacher
54. Ayurvedic Remedies from the Garden
55. Sages and Seers
56. Rising Strong – Motivational Stories of Women
57. Beyond Flames -Mystery stories of Funeral Ghat Manikarnika
58. The Origins of Tulsi: A Look at the Mythological Roots of the Plant"

Contact

DR. JAGADEESH PILLAI

PhD in Vedic Science

Four Times Guinness World Record Holder

Winner of Mahatma Gandhi Vishwa Shanti Puraskar and Global Peace Ambassador

Gemology, Astro & Vastu Consultant - Spiritual Counselor

Consultant for designing World Record Ideas

Efficient Tarot Card Reader

9839093003

myrichindia@gmail.com

drjagadeeshpillai@facebook

drjagadeeshpillai@instagram

jagadeeshpillai@youtube

www. JAGADEESHPILLAI.com

ॐ

|| LOKAHA SAMASTHAHA SUKHINO BHAVANTU ||